WITH THESE HANDS

WITH THESE HANDS

Photographs by Ken Light
Text by Paula DiPerna
Preface by Cesar Chavez

The Pilgrim Press, New York

The photographs in this book were made possible by grants to the photographer from the Max and Anna Levinson Foundation and the Rosenberg Foundation, a National Endowment for the Arts photographer's fellowship, and a National Endowment for the Arts survey grant. Research and travel for the writer were made possible by grants from the Ford Foundation, the Youth Project, the Ruth Mott Fund, and the Fund for Investigative Journalism.

Design by Henry Brimmer and Therese Randall.
Typography by Metrotype.
Printed by Phelps/Schaefer Lithographics.
Cover printed by Cal Central Press.

Printed in the United States of America.

Library of Congress Cataloging-in-Publication Data
Light, Ken.
With These Hands.

Bibliography: p.
1. Agricultural laborers – United States – Pictorial works. 2. Rural families – United States – Pictorial works. I. DiPerna, Paula. II. Title.
HD1525.L54   1986   331.7'63'0973   86-8152
ISBN 0-8298-0576-1 (pbk.)

The Pilgrim Press, 132 West 31st Street, New York, N.Y. 10001

Through these photographs I hope the viewer can see and feel a small part of the humanity of the people who "with these hands" daily contribute the labor that feeds America. Although these photographs will not compensate for years of neglect, my wish is for them to serve as a heartfelt cry that there remains among us a great injustice yet to be answered.

Acknowledgments

I would like to thank Stanley Light, who introduced me to photography, and Dorothea Light, who taught me to make my way. I would also like to thank the many friends and colleagues whose support, criticism, and confidence in me over these five years of image making have made this body of work possible. They are Roger Minick, Ed Levinson, Wayne Gibb, Morrie Camhi, Kirke Wilson, Fred Eyster, Carl Levinson, Carmen LiSing, Therese Randall, Henry Brimmer, Paul Raedeke, George Ortiz, Chauncey Hare, Pat Drydyk, Charles Horwitz, my editor, Susan C. Winslow, and Deanne Fitzmaurice. My thanks go also to the many unnamed campesinos who over the last five years let me into their lives and whose struggle, spirit, and humanity have inspired this book.

Ken Light

Royalties to the photographer and writer will be donated to the National Farm Worker Ministry, Oakland, California.

CONTENTS

PREFACE

It seems as though some things change and some things never do.

In 1963, on a lonely stretch of railroad track paralleling U.S. Highway 101 near Salinas, California, thirty-two bracero farm workers lost their lives in a tragic accident. The braceros were imported from Mexico to work on California farms. They died when their bus, which was converted from a flatbed truck, drove in front of a freight train. Conversion of the bus was not approved by any government agency. The driver was diagnosed as having tunnel vision. Most of the bodies lay unidentified for days. No one, including the grower who employed the workers, even knew their names.

Today, thousands of farm workers live under savage conditions beneath trees and brush in northern San Diego County and near Coachella—close to the luxurious swimming pools and well-tended golf courses of Palm Springs. They use irrigation water for bathing and cooking. Many carry drinking water in used pesticide containers.

Child labor is common in many farm areas. As many as 30 percent of northern California's garlic harvesters are children. Some 800,000 children work with their families harvesting crops in the United States.

Pesticide poisoning of food, and of the people who harvest it, are big concerns these days. And rightly so. Farm worker Juan Chavoya, thirty-two and the father of four children, was fatally stricken after laboring in a freshly sprayed field near San Diego on August 5, 1985. No one sought a doctor for him. He died in the field before the grower drove his body across the Mexican border and left it in Tijuana.

Situations like these are poignantly pictured in Ken Light's photographs in *With These Hands.* They are vividly evoked and clearly explained in Paula DiPerna's text. Together images and words present the humanity and dignity of the people who provide food for the tables of America.

Everything that we in the farm workers' movement have done has been driven by one dream, one goal, one vision: to overthrow a farm labor system in this nation that treats farm workers as if they are not important human beings. Farm workers are not agricultural implements. They are not beasts of burden to be used and discarded.

Our motivation springs from our personal lives, from watching what our parents went through when we were growing up as migrant farm workers. That dream, that vision, grew from our experience with racism, with hope, and with the desire to be treated fairly and to see our people treated as human beings, not as chattels.

It has been twenty years since our United Farm Workers first touched the hearts and consciences of people across America by letting them know about the abuses suffered by farm workers and their families.

Then we dramatically transformed the simple act of refusing to buy fresh grapes into a powerful statement against unfairness and injustice. The grape boycott, and similar boycotts that followed, were milestones in the 1960s and 1970s. They rallied millions of Americans to the cause of migrant farm workers. And they worked!

As a result, some farm workers now earn fair pay and have family medical plans, protection from dangerous pesticides, and paid holidays and vacations. Their children attend school, and they make enough to live in decent homes instead of rancid camps. Such achievements by the United Farm Workers are profiled in *With These Hands*.

But this progress for some farm workers only highlights the miserable poverty the great majority of farm workers still suffer in our midst. Abused workers in California saw their hopes for a better life shattered because Republican Governor George Deukmejian, elected with contributions of $1 million from corporate growers, won't enforce the farm labor law against those who break it.

California farm workers are once again placing their hopes for a better life in the American people's support for the boycott of fresh grapes not harvested by the UFW.

Exploitation of farm workers and their children is just as real today as it was twenty years ago. The fight is not over—it has just been renewed. You see, time does not heal injustice; only people do.

Cesar Chavez
President, United Farm Workers of America, AFL-CIO

OVERVIEW

The crusted earth of the cotton field crumbles under the hoe searching out weeds between cotton plants baked by the sun. Women, their teenage daughters, and elderly men make up the crew of hoers scratching at the soil in the Texas Panhandle. Their arms and spines ache from throwing the hoe before them and pulling it back, again and again, and the backs of their necks are burnt brown from so many similar days. At Hereford, Texas, cattle and vegetable country, there is no tree, no shade to relieve the sun beating down on the land. It stretches away flat, the heat rises in waves from fields and highways, and the stale smell of sweaty, grazing cattle and musty feed grain weighs in the air. There is no drinkable water, no toilet but an adjacent cornfield, no breaks from work except those taken without pay.

Against the moist, deep brown earth of Salinas, California, rows of leafy, sea-green lettuce seem to explode. They need thinning. A dozen men with faces like cracked mahogany under bell-shaped straw hats clear spaces between plants. One hunched man, small enough to be a boy, is sixty-eight years old; he remembers when farm workers in Salinas were glad to earn $2.50 a day.

Long, oval tomatoes lie like clumps of red and orange eggs in an Ohio field, which stretches auburn to the horizon except for blackened furrows, muddied by the rain. Workers bend to straddle the rows, tossing tomatoes with two hands into big plastic buckets. The steady thump, thump, thump is the only sound in the morning, the only refreshment the occasional splash of perspiration from one bare back to another as shirtless workers run down the rows to the waiting trucks to unload their buckets and back to the rows to start again.

1

Hands for Hire

Across the country, in fields such as these, more than 1 million hired farm workers, most of them poor, arduously plant, tend, and harvest the food crops that consumers easily buy in stores. Many of them are day laborers, who live with their families in agricultural areas the year round finding sporadic daily employment in nearby fields. Others are sharecroppers, who rent land to work in the hope that, after the landlord takes his share, there will be enough profit left over to support themselves and their families.

Most of the vegetable and fruit crops are harvested by migrant laborers, who, according to the Economic Research Service of the U.S. Department of Agriculture, made up 9 percent of hired farm workers in 1983. Some are single men or men who have left their families behind while they travel about in search of work. Often, however, whole families, as many as three generations together, pack their belongings into aged cars and trucks and follow the growing season and the crops in a cyclical pursuit of work. In general, migrants work in southern areas in winter, where the crops grow all year, and move north following the path of summer. There are several distinct migrant "streams" from south to north, traveled year after year. Some migrants base themselves in southern California and make up the stream that heads north to Oregon and Washington. Others, based in Texas and Arizona, travel up the Mississippi Valley to Ohio, Michigan, Indiana, and Illinois. Still others move from southern Florida up through Georgia, the Carolinas, Maryland, Delaware, and New Jersey into New York and New England.

Many farm workers are lone men from outside the United States imported for a season by growers who claim they cannot find local laborers. At the end of the season they are sent home.

Finally, there are the undocumented, the thousands of workers, mostly men, who enter the United States illegally every year. As the latest arrivals, they occupy the lowest rung of the farm-worker ladder. No one knows how many there really are. It is roughly estimated that there are several million undocumented workers of all kinds, including farm workers. Most are recent arrivals from Latin America. Usually they speak little or no English. The Mexicans and Central Americans secretly cross the U.S. border, often under the auspices of "coyotes," who charge high fees for getting them into the United States. Frequently, the undocumented carry no possessions other than the clothes they wear and perhaps a jug of water. In states such as

Cabbage field
Rio Grande Valley, Texas 1979

Arizona, where many of them find their first jobs, they are not even provided miserable camps to live in but instead are left to fend for themselves once they are beyond the area where La Migra–the Immigration Service–is on patrol. They build caves in the sides of hills or huts from scrap wood or sheets of plastic. They are trapped on the land they work, without friends, without money, without a driver's licence, without means to leave, while basics such as shelter and water are denied them.

Ironically, most of these aliens have entered the United States in the hope of making a better life than was possible in their native countries. Here they live in constant fear of being sent home. Stories circulate among them, for example, of growers who, after the season's picking is done, report the workers to Immigration for deportation in order to avoid paying the wages due them. Fear of economic deprivation in their homeland, and for some of them, of political repression as well, keeps the undocumented worker silent and compliant.

Today farm workers in the United States represent the ethnic groups of two hemispheres: whites, blacks, Chicanos, Jamaicans, Haitians, Puerto Ricans, Mexicans, Guatemalans, Salvadorans, Vietnamese, Laotians, Cambodians, Filipinos. Increasingly, they are refugees from civil wars. They are employed by both small farmers and large corporate agricultural producers all around the country. And they not only pick, but plant, carry, haul, climb, hoe, weed, pack, carry, and count. Though mechanization of field work has contributed to a large decline in the overall number of workers needed, most crops—among them strawberries, onions, cabbage, potatoes, tomatoes, tobacco, cucumbers, garlic, and sugar cane—still require manual work. One crop comes into season as another goes out, and workers head where they think they will be needed.

Whatever their category or ethnic origin, most farm workers share the same dreary working conditions—low wages for brutally tiring work; dirty, ramshackle housing, often with no indoor plumbing; poor field sanitation; fatigue and poor health from constant heavy labor and exposure to pesticides; no health insurance; no unemployment insurance; no fringe benefits; and always, no rest. For fear of being replaced or deported, most labor silently, gratefully accepting heavy work, low payment, and less thanks.

Although the tide of public interest in the sad saga of the farm workers rises and falls, actual conditions have changed little over the years. Despite what is now decades of public awareness about the plight of farm workers, victories are still slow and small. It took fifty years to win the battle of the short-handled hoe, that is, in some states winning the right to use hoes with long handles like brooms rather than short handles little longer than trowels. Relief from bending, thanks to a few feet of handle–that is one of the incremental gains by which farm workers measure their progress.

The battle of the hoe is only one small part of the farm workers' struggle. There are also the battles for decent wages, a decent place to sleep at night, safety on the job, and access to the laws that are supposed to provide such things. In these battles, farm workers embrace both the pain of work and the pride of life, maintaining dignity in the face of working conditions that any thoughtful society should find unacceptable. It is this staunch human spirit, despite what is sometimes the pure futility of struggle, that inspires the telling of the farm workers' story again and again.

The Demand for Seasonal Labor

The farm workers depend on the farm owners' need for seasonal labor. According to agricultural economist Stephen H. Sosnick in his *Hired Hands: Seasonal Farm Workers in the United States* (1978), seasonal farm work for wages began to be common in the middle of the nineteenth century. In those years, farms were becoming increasingly specialized. Farmers devoted large tracts of land to wheat or some other one crop, which ripened at one season, rather than cultivating many different crops with harvest seasons staggered through the year. Consequently they needed many workers for a short time only once a year. As the economist Paul Taylor described it, "In deciding what to plant in the Spring, men began to turn away from mixed farming–the traditional balance of crops adjusted to family.... The laborers sought were no longer 'hired men' engaged for the year to work steadily, each one beside a working farmer; now they were extra hands wanted at harvest time only."

The need for seasonal help was particularly great in California, where there were large wheat farms and a shortage of native-born workers. Wheat farmers hired as the first seasonal workers Chinese immigrants who settled in the West after working on the railroads and other construction projects. The farmers' dependence on the Chinese was similar to the dependence of white Southern planters on black slaves before the Civil War.

The poor working and living conditions of these seasonal laborers, despite their reluctance to complain, were not unnoticed. An agrarian reformer in 1880 told the California State Agricultural Society about the dangers of large-scale farming dependent on wage labor: "Such farming as this may enrich the particular owner but it introduces a feudal system. It makes the State a wilderness, and brings society back to the barbarism of the medieval age. It destroys homes and the family. It breeds tramps and idlers. It destroys churches and school-houses. It would in time present the green, beautiful valleys of our State as treeless, verdureless plains."

Such warnings notwithstanding, crop specialization went on. When vast irrigation projects made it possible to transform desert tracts into fertile gardens, such as the San Joaquin Valley, California became one of the country's leading producers of fruits and vegetables, crops that greatly increased the demand for seasonal labor. Growers further specialized in one type of crop, which meant that workers could not stay in one place but had to move north with the season, as different crops matured at different times. Diversification of crops, which would have reduced the sharp peak-and-fall, seasonal quality of work, would have meant a significant loss in the value of the crops produced by each acre of land, so specialization continued.

In the early twentieth century, California growers used Japanese and Indian immigrants for farm work, augmented by Mexicans, who came north after the Mexican Revolution. The Immigration Laws of 1921 and 1924, however, restricted the flow of Asians to the United States. Experiencing a shortage of foreign labor willing to work for low wages, the growers began to call for easterners to come farm the Promised Land. Many eastern and midwestern farmers, burdened by poor soil, drought, and especially the Great Depression of the 1930s, sold their land and headed west.

After World War II, growers in California, Texas, and other states began to import Mexican workers legally under the federal government's bracero program, during the 1950s about half a million a year. In theory the program provided foreign workers for jobs for which domestic workers could not be found. It was very controversial, however, in that by swelling the supply of workers, it kept wages low. When the program was discontinued in 1964, poor and unemployed Mexican citizens, known condescendingly as wetbacks, began to enter the United

States illegally in unprecedented numbers. They have been coming ever since, despite government efforts to prevent or deport them.

The bracero program, however, lived on in a different form, called the H-2 program, which allows growers, particularly of apples and sugar cane, to import workers legally on a short-term basis when they can "prove" domestic workers are not available. Under this federal program, about 15,000 black Jamaican and Haitian men—assumed to be tough, experienced cutters with no employment possibilities at home—are brought to the United States each year. They earn between $4,500 and $6,500 for a season cutting sugar cane. In Florida, 70 percent of the sugar cane crop is cut by imported workers. Wielding a machete in the heat against the tough stalks of cane is hard work. According to an article in the *Wall Street Journal* in January 1985, "No white man in 25 years has completed the six-month cane-cutting season. Only a handful since World War II have tried." If sugar cane growers paid higher wages, unquestionably they would find sufficient domestic workers.

The Burdens of Farm Work

For all farm workers, the opportunity to work is the prize, but the prize is subject to vagaries well beyond the workers' control. Bad weather is a curse, for it means crops might be damaged and therefore there will be less work and less pay. A drop in market prices is a curse because it means a grower may let a crop rot in the field rather than pick it at a loss. Machines are a curse because, though they make work easier, they mean fewer hands are hired and there is less work overall. Unionization too is considered a curse by some because it means a farmer will simply hire "others," who make fewer demands. "Others" are always among the farm workers; they are those who are even less well off than the merely badly off. Farm workers, therefore—whether migrant, day laborers, sharecroppers, importees, or undocumented—epitomize vulnerability, for they are a supply in search of demand. As such they are ready victims for exploitation.

Chits
forty buckets at 35¢ each
Homestead, Florida 1982

Low Pay

The most obvious form of exploitation is low pay. By and large farmers set the wages they will pay from one season to another, orchestrating the pay scale among neighboring farmers, depending on market prices and the availability of workers. Lowering of wages spreads like fire from farm to farm, and if there is little work, workers generally accept what they are offered.

Accurate figures are hard to come by, but some may be offered. In 1965 grape workers in California were receiving roughly $1.20 an hour, more than the farm-worker minimum wage of $1.00 an hour but less than the nonfarm minimum of $1.40. In 1966, a study of migrant workers in Washington state found that the typical migrant worked 8.6 hours a day, was paid $1.46 per hour, and had an annual income from agricultural work of $1,200 and a total annual income of about $2,300, according to Congressional hearings in 1969. In 1975, according to the Economic Research Service, annual cash wages for migratory heads of household were $5,216, minus traveling expenses. In 1981, the average migrant worker earned $27 a day and worked 98 days a year, for an average annual income from farm work of about $2,600, as reported by Philip L. Martin in *Scientific American* (October 1983). The average annual income from farm work for a migrant family of four in 1983 was estimated at $4,600 to $4,800, according to the latest figures available from the Economic Research Service.

Sometimes it is difficult for most farm workers to know what they are actually being paid. In most situations, they are covered by minimum-wage laws, but these are calculated in hours. Farm workers are often paid by the piece or the box or the acre—so many heads of lettuce, so many flats of strawberries, so many acres of cucumbers. Consequently, workers, or their crew leaders, must calculate the salary, dividing the money they receive on a piecework basis by the hours worked in order to determine if minimum wage has been met. In tomatoes, for example, workers can be paid thirty-five to forty cents for a full thirty-five-pound-capacity bucket, or a cent or less a pound. A family of six working an eight-hour day can sometimes pick four hundred to five hundred buckets, earning between $140 and $175 a day, for $2.91 to $3.64 per person per hour.

A male worker in top physical condition considers fifteen buckets an hour to be record money, which works out to $6.00 an hour, but even the most hardy worker cannot keep up that pace very long. A more typical full day of work for an average male is forty buckets, at thirty-five cents each, or $14. And the work does not go on all year but for only a fraction of it. According to Sosnick, calculations show that farm workers in the 1970s had about 8 percent fewer workdays per year than the average for other American workers, and they earned roughly half what manufacturing workers earned for comparable time.

Child Labor

The lamentable level of pay has often meant that, especially among migrants, whole families must work, including grandparents and children. Child labor has long been an integral part of farm work, particularly in fruit and vegetable table crops, which require careful hand labor and tend to be harvested by migrant workers.

Dr. Robert Coles wrote in his book *Migrants, Sharecroppers, and Mountaineers* (1970), "To my eye, migrant children begin a migrant life very, very early. By and large they are allowed rather free rein as soon as they can begin to crawl. Even before that they do not usually have cribs and often enough they lack clothes and usually toys of any sort. Put differently, the migrant child learns right off that he has no particular possessions of his own, no place that is his to use for rest and sleep, no objects that are his to look at and touch and move about and come to recognize as familiar."

The situation has improved somewhat for migrant children, largely because some migrant families have over the years earned enough to establish "permanent," albeit simple, homes in the south, and they come north toward the end of the school year. But summer for any migrant child still means work in the fields. Federal law prohibits the hiring of children under twelve for farm work, but this law is not always enforced and can easily be violated. It often is by parents who need the money their children can earn to meet family expenses.

**Young pickers and infant
Northwest Ohio 1980**

Poor Housing

Substandard housing, sometimes provided "free," is another curse for farm workers. Often housing is deplorable; frequently it is simply dirty. Always, though, it is barely basic. Any traveler in agricultural America can see long, low barracks-style shacks and cabins adjacent to fields–sometimes made of wood, sometimes of cement blocks or metal roofing materials. Rooms frequently contain many cots jammed tightly together. Toilets are communal, as are bathrooms. Potable water usually comes from one source, frequently an outdoor pump. Walls are either unpainted wood or exposed cement blocks.

According to *The Tidings*, the newspaper of the Roman Catholic Archdiocese of Los Angeles (Oct. 4, 1985), Bishop Thaddeus Shubsda found living conditions in ranches north of Salinas "appalling and subhuman." Some workers were living in holes burrowed into the ground in a eucalyptus grove. Others found shelter in small wooden shacks, old partitioned delivery trucks, leaky barns, boxes, and latrines turned on their sides.

In other places one can see such things as cardboard sheets stuffed into openings in walls, with the words "Fire Exit" handwritten on them; screens repaired with rolled up paper napkins; and mattresses stained seasons before, their stuffing bursting like puffed wheat from many small tears. "These people," said one Ohio farmer, "ruin the camps themselves. They don't know how to be clean." But such statements blame the victims for conditions they find unchanged year after year.

Lack of Field Sanitation

Poor sanitation in the fields makes them among the country's most uncomfortable workplaces. Most of the time, there is no fresh water to drink, unless workers themselves bring it along in a cooler or thermos jug. Most importantly, there are almost never toilet facilities. Very occasionally, fields are equipped with portable toilets, but usually workers must either leave the field and return to camp to use facilities–with concomitant loss of pay–or find some privacy in the fields themselves. When an official of the National Farm Worker Ministry asked a woman picking oranges in a Florida grove why she wore a long skirt over blue jeans, she replied, "It's the only privacy I have when I go to the bathroom." There is no federal standard requiring growers to provide workers with basic field sanitation, and there are few such standards at state levels.

Pesticide Poisoning

Illness caused by exposure to pesticides continually plagues farm workers. The first national attention to the problem was paid in the Congressional hearings of 1969 and 1970, which devoted several sessions to the subject. Testimony was given at the time that the number of doctors' reports on pesticide-related illnesses had doubled since 1951, that California alone had between 800 to 1,000 reports annually, and that farm workers were considered to be at significant risk.

Today the situation remains largely unchanged. According to a report by the World Resources Institute, released in July 1985, the health of more than 300,000 farm workers a year in the United States is adversely affected by exposure to pesticides. With the banning in the United States of many of the most toxic and long-lived organochlorine chemicals, such as DDT and aldrin, agriculture increased its use of another group, the organophosphates, which break down and dissipate more quickly in the field but which are more acutely toxic and need to be applied to crops more often. They act on humans by depressing body blood levels of the enzyme cholinesterase. Without enough cholinesterase, another enzyme, the neurochemical acetylcholine, accumulates at junctions of brain cells. This interference with brain chemicals can cause a variety of symptoms about which farm workers often complain—including nausea, vomiting, cramps, twitching, frequent urination, and dizziness. Rashes and other skin problems are commonly associated with direct contact with pesticides, and many pesticides are also known or suspected to cause cancer and birth defects among humans or laboratory animals.

Farm workers can be exposed in several ways. One is obvious—a study by the Florida Rural Legal Service in May 1980 found that 40 percent of four hundred workers surveyed could report having been sprayed at least once directly while they were at work in the fields as a result of careless application of pesticide by specially hired pesticide sprayers or the growers themselves. Field workers also touch pesticide residue on plants and in dirt, and they inhale vapors that can linger for days after chemicals have been applied. In addition they risk direct exposure through drift from ground spray rigs or overhead planes, for sprays rise up over the plants and drift across rows like puffs of low clouds or lifting fog, even when there is no wind.

Workers can also suffer pesticide poisoning simply by entering a field that has been directly sprayed. Except for Monterey County in California, no county in the United States requires that fields be posted with signs to advise workers when a field was last sprayed or with what; there is no provision for what a farm worker called "a Beware of Dog sign that says what kind of dog and if it will bite."

There is important information, known as the reentry time interval, which means the time that must elapse after the application of a given pesticide before humans can return to the area. As of 1985 the Environmental Protection Agency had established safe reentry standards for only a handful of chemicals, so often reentry times are left to the best guess of the farmer, based on experience, even though pesticides can behave unpredictably, depending on the crop and the weather conditions.

Relying on experience, a grower sent a crew of eighteen workers, including three children under twelve and their seventy-two-year-old grandfather, into a field in Salinas, California, in July 1980 to band cauliflower leaves to the plant heads. The field had been sprayed with Phosdrin and phosphamidon, both organophosphates, and no worker should have entered the field until at least seventy-two hours had passed. But because of what the grower later called a "breakdown in communications," workers were told to begin banding. Shortly thereafter, most of them, including the children, were suffering from nausea and dizziness, blurred vision, and headaches. Some were hospitalized.

There was a virtual replay in another field the next year, as well as in Samsula, Florida, in May 1985, when a farmer accompanied ten local adolescents into a field of collard greens to begin picking. Soon they were all hospitalized with acute pesticide poisoning–dizziness, blurred vision, fainting, and nausea–because the field had been sprayed several days earlier with Phosdrin. The farmer said, "I've been using this chemical on and off for twenty-five years and never had this problem. I thought I had waited long enough."

As a result of these and other numerous pesticide-related complaints, pressure has built to require field posting nationwide. Even in Monterey County, however, there are shortcomings in signposting guidelines, since the signs need not be dated nor a specific chemical

**Crop duster
Rio Grande Valley, Texas 1979**

named. The printing wears off the signs, and workers then ignore them, unsure whether they still apply. For the farm worker is always inclined to live by the rule, "When in doubt, work."

Apart from the problem of acute poisoning, there is the question of chronic ill effects related to extended contact with, and ingestion of, highly toxic substances. Children especially sometimes eat some of what they or their parents pick. Since fresh water in the field, with which to wash away the dirt of work before eating, is almost never provided, unless the workers bring their own, they frequently drink from irrigation troughs, which can carry water contaminated with fertilizers and which are sometimes themselves used to distribute pesticides to plants. Since portable toilets are rarities in the fields, farm workers must use bushes or trees. And if workers do not carry toilet paper or Kleenex, they often use leaves, sometimes recently sprayed, and the genital areas are known to have extremely high rates of chemical absorption.

Discarded empty pesticide containers are the pottery of labor camps, used for everything from flower pots for a few red geraniums to carriers for drinking water, from garbage cans to seats. They are even used, with bottoms cut out, as hoops for basketball games. The containers are supposed to be disposed of in special landfills for toxic wastes, but many containers lie abandoned beside the fields. Label warnings are printed mostly in English, which many workers do not read, with the result that discarded containers are used by those who do not know better. In one camp, a child put her bare feet inside two empty pesticide buckets and whirled them around her ankles for fun. In short, the lamentable lack of hygienic facilities in the field and in labor camps and the lack of awareness of the hazard only worsen the danger of pesticide-related illness.

Unscrupulous Crew Leaders

Already struggling against low pay and poor living and working conditions, many farm workers must also protect themselves against the often unscrupulous practices of those who are go-betweens in securing work. Rather than deal with individual workers, many growers use a farm-labor contractor, or crew leader, usually an independent person who takes responsibility for recruiting the workers the grower needs. The crew leader also transports them to the work site, records their productivity, and distributes their wages. Some crew leaders migrate with their workers; others stay put and wait for workers to arrive. Others specialize in day-haul work in rural areas. Still others collect usually homeless city men and bring them to work in the fields. Generally, crew leaders are paid directly by the growers and receive commissions often exceeding 25 percent of the workers' wages.

As one might expect, there are good and bad crew leaders. In September 1983, the House of Representatives Subcommittee on Labor Standards of the Committee on Education and Labor held hearings on the question of peonage and indentured servitude among agricultural workers. Testimony was given by local church personnel against crew leaders in North Carolina, who had kidnaped and brutalized workers, holding them in camps against their will. The committee heard of a group of approximately thirty Haitians who had been brought to the United States under contract to a crew leader, who then expelled the workers from his camp without paying them the wages due.

Migrants, too, must often contend with crew leaders, both men and women, who may be dishonest in reporting wages, or who insist their crews buy food or other supplies through them at high prices. At Ruskin, Florida, a white crew leader with close-cropped blonde hair talked through the barbed wire camp fence. Men and their families gathered silently behind him. He fingered a greasy piece of chicken and answered, "I dunno" to every question about how many workers he had hired, when they would start work, and what they would be paid. The families had come to pick tomatoes, and they were settling into camp, their yellow foam mattresses popping out to full length after having been bunched inside cars for many miles. The farmer who had hired the leader to recruit the workers had not yet begun picking his crop, and so the workers would have to wait. "I'll just let them lay out for awhile," said the crew leader, though the workers would not be paid for this waiting time.

Crew leaders are often former field workers who have made their way up the fieldwork hierarchy and who are glad at last to have a taste of power. They lapse into the language of those in control. Just as growers call their crew leaders demeaningly "these people," crew leaders call their crews "these people." Whites call blacks "these people," blacks call Hispanics "these people," and Hispanic crew leaders, increasingly in charge of Asian workers, call them "these people." Somehow, "these people" always seem less human to those who use the term.

Undocumented workers
Orange grove
Salt River Valley, Arizona 1979

Silence

Both documented and undocumented workers are reluctant to report abuses in the fields, and workers keep an unspoken compact, by and large, to mind their own business. When a stranger enters the field, all workers look down quickly, burying their eyes in the plants as if hoping to become invisible. Workers seem to want to disappear before strangers, for in the fields, any stranger could be an inspector who wants to talk, and for farm workers talk almost never means anything good. Immigration inspectors might want to talk about undocumented workers—in Florida alone, 1,400 men were arrested and deported in 1982 to their country of origin. Labor Department inspectors want to talk about wages, but complaints could get back to the "bossman" and so workers do not complain because they do not want to lose their jobs. Health officials might want to talk about illness, but a worker who confesses to having rashes or headaches or to feeling dizzy will be removed from the field and thus be out of work. Because talk—of whatever kind—can lead to no money, nobody talks.

Pressures of the Farm Economy

The intractable nature of the farm workers' plight cannot be divorced from constraints on the farm economy or from the situation of the farmers themselves. Small farmers, and their hired seasonal help, each dependent on the other, are trapped by the harsh demands of the U.S. agricultural system. As pressure intensifies on small farmers to find ways to stay in business, as a result of increasing debt and decreasing value for the equity they have in their land and equipment, farmers often have little choice other than to cut away at workers' wages and monies spent on workers' benefits. The workers then are often given the stark choice of work or don't work—take it or leave it.

Most farm costs—land taxes, fertilizers, heavy equipment, packing crates—are fixed, if not on the rise. So the only place to cut costs is on labor, and it is relatively easy to lower the piece rate for a flat of cherries or a bucket of tomatoes. Workers who have traveled far to a job are unlikely to turn it down once they arrive.

And there is an anonymous "they" in farming, those in the middle on whom the farmer depends to distribute and sell the crops. In Ruskin, for example, plump tomatoes hung from wooden stakes in the field like gleaming wax balls about to melt. They were ready to pick, but, a farmer said, "I'm going to lose the tomatoes if I don't pick 'em, and lose money if I do—there's just no price for them right now." By that he meant that the wholesale price had plunged to ten cents a pound. The farmer had spent that amount just on land taxes, seed, fertilizers, fumigants, plastic tarp, and other supplies. He expected to spend another nine and a half cents a pound to pick, pack, and ship the crop. For smallish tomatoes, there was so little hope of breaking even that they were just rolled down the chute in the packing shed into the garbage. The farmer pointed out, "We pay our workers by the pound, but we get paid by the size."

And he added a comment about the middlemen, "They know we have to pick now, even though there is no price, because we have no place to store tomatoes. So they get our first pick, the cream of the crop, for nothing. They hold 'em up there and sell 'em high when they get a good demand."

In California, when the cherry tomato crop comes in, and the tomatoes are too ripe to survive shipment to the northeast, sometimes the price plunges so low that growers tell the workers to take the tomatoes home, rather than pick them and charge the growers for the time. And in Yakima, Washington, while Yakima asparagus cutters were earning fifteen cents a pound, or $4 for a forty-pound box, California asparagus were retailing in the Yakima supermarkets for ninety-nine cents a pound. It is a system that says food cannot be profitably consumed where it is grown, and that the price of plentiful production is low profit for those who produce.

Many farmers grow hostile when people whom they call "do gooders" make inquiries about people whom the farmers call "the labor." Most farmers simply do not agree that farm workers suffer exploitation at all. As one county extension agent of the state Agricultural Department in Ohio put it, explaining why corn fields were planted around the tomato fields, "That is to keep the goddamn public from seeing the supposedly poor migrant labor, and you can quote me on that."

Some farmers argue that they pay a fair day's wage for a fair day's work, and that it is the farm workers who do not work hard enough or who leave the job before their contracts expire and therefore do not earn a full living.

Many farmers seem bitter, for they feel victimized themselves and dislike being cast as villains. One farmer, a likable, hardworking man in Ohio, sat relaxedly in an executive swivel chair in his office. He was better off than his workers but still no tycoon. His days were long, and his income and efforts for a year could be wiped out by one ferocious storm. He was outraged that vandals from a nearby city had driven their car into one of his best fields, crushing melons he was getting ready to harvest, "just for the fun of it," he said.

Yet, he was full of subtle and unsubtle prejudices. In the course of otherwise pleasant conversation he complained about the electric bill to heat water in one of his labor camps, commenting, "I always say a Mexican never takes a bath until he comes to Ohio" or "Blacks—all they do is multiply."

In 1985, a number of agricultural employers associations, representing growers, successfully lobbied to prevent the establishment of a federal standard for field sanitation, which would have required portable field toilets, even though complying with the law would have cost only fifty-five to seventy-five cents a day per worker.

Advocates for farm workers argue that farmers could recover costs incurred to pay better wages and improve housing conditions by raising their wholesale prices, given that the average American family spends a relatively small percentage of income on food compared to most other developed countries. Farmers are not so sure, however, particularly farmers who sell their crops to one main buyer. For example, farmers in the Toledo, Ohio, area sell their tomato and cucumber crops to large catsup and other food processors, who set prices in advance of the crops' having even been planted. That means that no matter how much costs increase over the growing season—for fertilizer, pesticides, labor—the farmer's gross income is predetermined. A farmer may then justifiably lament, "How can we make these canneries pay more than they are willing to pay? They can get what they need in paste from California if our prices go too high."

These same farmers are also squeezed by the need to obtain higher crop yields from each acre planted. They therefore buy expensive large machines to make producing large crops easier, incurring debt essentially by playing the wholesale and retail food market, and as a result, extinguishing jobs for workers.

Rising Concern and Protective Legislation

As the Depression hit in the 1930s, farm workers attempted to achieve some semblance of rights and security of income. Their efforts took the form of strikes, riots, and violence, which drew national attention to their wretched plight. John Steinbeck dramatically and realistically chronicled the struggles of those years in his masterly novel *The Grapes of Wrath* (1939). The U.S. Farm Security Administration sent out photographers such as Walker Evans, Arthur Rothstein, Russell Lee, Marion Post Wolcott, Dorothea Lange, and Carl Mydens to document the poverty of many rural areas. It built temporary shelters for migrants in 1939 and 1940.

In 1939 the LaFollette Committee opened hearings in San Francisco to investigate denial of civil liberties to farm workers. At the hearings, however, Steinbeck was denounced as "the arch-enemy and defamer of migratory farm labor" by the Associated Farmers Annual Convention, who also told Senator LaFollette of Wisconsin to go home and stop "giving aid and comfort to the Communists." This incident was related by Carey McWilliams in one of his many books about farmwork, *Ill Fares the Land* (1942). McWilliams himself was called "Agricultural Pest No. 1 in California, outranking pear blight and boll weevil."

In 1960 the classic documentary *Harvest of Shame* by Edward R. Murrow appeared on television. With that event the farm workers' plight was no longer a matter of words written by some that others could discredit but of undeniable visual images seen by a wide audience. The exploitation exposed by Murrow stimulated a flurry of national outrage. Congress established the Senate Subcommittee on Migratory Labor and began to put in place a network of laws intended to right a long list of wrongs.

The first of these laws was the Migrant Health Act of 1962. It provided for a series of clinics for farm workers and for other facilities that would offer health care to migrant workers at nominal cost. The Economic Opportunity Act (OEA) of 1964 provided for day care for migrants' children and authorized new programs under the Farmers' Home Administration that improved housing for migrant workers. Long-term loans and grants were given to growers to build housing for migrants according to government standards. The money was used chiefly for large, low buildings of two-room flats, which included a cold-water sink, bathroom, and

**Onion picker
Rio Grande Valley, Texas 1979**

outlets for electricity and gas. Funds were also made available to migrants to help them buy, rent, or build houses for themselves. More than 10,000 families were enabled to build their own homes.

The Elementary and Secondary Education Act (ESEA) of 1965 established national programs to compensate for the education of disadvantaged children, including specific provision for children of migrant workers. Individual states are helped to offer special services to these children so that they do not lose school time as they move from one school district to another. For example, in Texas, classes start in November and meet from 8:00 to 5:00 so that children can have a full school program that finishes in the spring. In some parts of Louisiana, school is held only in the afternoons so that the children can work in the fields in the morning. The act also includes the Migrant Student Record Transfer System (MSRTS), which distributes both educational and health records of migrant children so that if they do move around mid-year, they are not in a position of starting from scratch each time. The High School Equivalency Program (HEP), funded by the federal government, holds classes for migrant workers' children, which enable them to qualify for a General Education Development diploma, but it doesn't reach many children. As a result of these educational measures, some modest progress has been made, but the efforts are inadequate in face of the great continuing need.

The Farm Labor Contractor Registration Act (FLCRA) was passed in 1965. Its aim was to lessen the level of abuses by crew leaders. It provided that payroll records be posted, with a full explanation of deductions that the crew leader had made, including a clear explanation of what the penalties would be if the worker failed to complete the contract. The act also required crew leaders to be licensed and to renew their license annually.

After 1965 with the increasing unionization of farm workers and the launching of President Lyndon Johnson's "war on poverty," awareness of the problems of farm workers intensified. Congress conducted a long series of hearings titled "Migrant and Seasonal Farm Worker Powerlessness" in 1969 and 1970. The American Friends Service Committee did a study of child labor in 1970. The reforms embodied in existing legislation were extended and made more effective. Clinics were expanded and included dental care, and housing provisions improved. FLCRA was toughened in 1979 and in 1983 was replaced by the Migrant and Seasonal Agricultural Workers' Protection Act (MSAWPA). Both laws make employers liable for violations by crew leaders.

A new concern was the harmful effects on workers of pesticides used in the fields. The Federal Insecticide, Fungicide, and Rodenticide Act (FIFRA), passed in 1947, is the major national legislation controlling the use of pesticides, but it makes no direct reference to the specific conditions farm workers face in the field. FIFRA was amended by the Federal Environment Pesticide Control Act (FEPCA) in 1972, which makes it illegal to send workers into a field treated with pesticides before the reentry time has passed, but since few reentry standards have been set, farm workers are afforded little protection. Since the 1970s a coalition of labor, environmental, and consumer groups has been working to have FIFRA strengthed.

To ease the cost of travel, the federal government operates an overnight "rest stop" in Hope, Arkansas, for migrants in the Texas to Middle West stream. There, enroute betweeen their winter homes and their work, for twenty-five cents farm workers can find clean, overnight shelter and a hot bath, as well as cooking facilities. The shelter serves some 2,000 farm workers, mostly migrant families, during its peak periods in June and September, and serves approximately 35,000 workers a year.

In addition to these federal measures, individual states have a battery of laws covering farm workers, which supplement the body of federal law. California leads in innovative approaches to protecting farm workers, as evidenced by the passage in 1985 of stricter legislation on protection against pesticides and on field posting.

There are problems, however, with enforcement. Although migrant housing is supposed to meet minimum health standards, one hears of typhoid epidemics in camps. Although migrants are supposed to be protected from pesticides, one hears of poisonings. Although wages are supposed to be fairly paid, one hears of violations of wage guidelines.

Enforcement can be only as effective as the willingness and ability to enforce. There are too few enforcement officers and too many hidden camps, too many fields, and too many workers moving around too much for more than scant enforcement. And often workers may be stranded away from home, with no access to a telephone from which to report an abuse, even if they knew to which agency to report it. Justice in the fields slips through the fingers like a handful of soil.

To attempt to provide farm workers with better access to legal aid and enforcement possibilities, through the Office of Economic Opportunity, the Legal Services program was established in the mid 1960s. It was eventually transferred to the Legal Services Corporation,

Tomato picker
waiting for the pick-up
Immokalee, Florida 1982

when the Office of Economic Opportunity was dismantled in 1973. The corporation funds the Migrant Legal Action Program, a national support center that provides assistance to Legal Services attorneys and the private bar when representing migrant farm workers who are eligible for those services, particularly in matters relating to working and living conditions. Again, the California Rural Legal Assistance office has been a leader in the area. It was criticized in the late 1960s by then Governor Ronald Reagan for using federal funds to sue the state and federal government for not enforcing existing laws.

However, the rural migrant legal services programs have been an important voice for farm workers, and there have been several cases of particular note. One involved a female grape worker in Delano, California, who gave birth to a limbless child. She had worked in the fields during her pregnancy and had been exposed to a number of pesticides, including the fungicide captan, which is similar chemically to thalidomide, the drug that was shown to cause serious birth defects involving lack of limb development. After a number of years of studying the effects of captan residue, in June 1985, the Environmental Protection Agency (EPA) proposed that it be banned for use on food products because of its potential for causing cancer in laboratory animals.

Farm Workers' Unions

Of course, a farm worker should not have to begin a court action every time his or her basic rights have been violated, or whenever he or she has suffered some harm. But traditionally, the other avenue that workers have used to settle grievances, unions, has not been available to farm workers.

In 1935, when the National Labor Relations Act was passed, which gave most workers the right to unionize and have their unions accepted as bona fide negotiating bodies by employers, the act specifically excluded agricultural workers. Some gestures were made on behalf of farm workers by such groups as the Southern Tenant Farmer's Union, founded in Arkansas by H.L. Mitchell in 1934, and Local 56 of the Food and Commercial Workers' Union in Camden,

New Jersey, in the 1940s. Ernest Galarza organized grape pickers in the DiGiorgio strike of 1947 in California. The International Longshoreman and Warehouse Workers' Union (ILWU) had contracts with growers in Hawaii that covered some field workers. None of these groups, however, succeeded in attracting large numbers of farm workers or winning long-term contracts.

In 1959 a group called the Agricultural Workers' Organizing Committee (AWOC) was formed at the suggestion of such labor leaders as Walter Reuther of the United Automobile Workers. AWOC organizers galvanized some farm workers to strike to call attention to poor conditions in the early 1960s. They also criticized the bracero program because they thought that importing laborers who would accept low pay kept the wages down for citizens as well. The growers did not recognize the committee, however, and it won no contracts.

At about the same time, Cesar Chavez, a young man who had grown up in California and was a farm worker himself, began to think about uniting farm workers into a service organization. He had had experience working in community affairs with the Community Service Organization, which had been formed to secure civil rights, such as voting, for Mexican-Americans. In 1962 the thirty-five-year-old Chavez gathered other interested farm workers to his cause. The group went from house to house in small towns and labor camps addressing such problems as the lack of Social Security for farm workers and objecting to the bracero program. As interest grew among workers, Chavez formed the National Farm Workers Association (NFWA) and established a credit union, as well as a group insurance program to cover unexpected expenses, such as funeral costs, that farm workers' families had no way of meeting. By 1965, roughly 1,700 farm workers' families had begun paying dues to the Chavez-led organization.

At roughly the same time, the Teamsters Union had also begun trying to organize agricultural workers. It even had some contracts with growers setting minimum labor conditions for employees who worked in the packing and canning sheds. When the Teamsters began to try to add field workers to their ranks, there was at first some territorial squabbling between the Teamsters and the NFWA about who had the right to speak for the workers in the field.

In 1965 the grape pickers in California's San Joaquin Valley went on strike. Several months later the NFWA called for a boycott of grapes from that region as a means of drawing attention to the workers' plight. The boycott also meant that the union attempted to induce consumers not to buy the grapes as a way of putting pressure on growers to recognize the union and improve farm workers' conditions. Such boycotts eventually were extended to include lettuce and other crops. There were also battles and intimidation, although Chavez consistently advocated that the union should have a nonviolent approach. In 1966, the National Farm Worker Association joined with the Agricultural Workers Committee under the auspices of the American Federation of Labor and Congress of Industrial Organizations (AFL-CIO) and became the United Farm Worker Organizing Committee (UFWOC). At this point, the new UFWOC reached an agreement with the Teamsters Union that UFWOC exclusively would represent field workers.

Chavez' achievement was that for the first time large numbers of farm workers were speaking for themselves and winning recognition in the form of long-term contracts. Since then Chavez has become an internationally recognized labor figure, and the UFWOC has grown into the United Farm Workers union (UFW). Its strongest base remains in California, although UFW-supported unionizing efforts have sporadically taken place in such states as Florida among citrus workers and Texas among vegetable workers.

Other people have attempted to unionize farm workers. Perhaps the most successful new effort has been in Ohio in the 1980s by Baldemar Velasquez, head of the Farm Labor Organizing Committee (FLOC). Working out of a small office at the top of some rickety stairs in Toledo, FLOC has organized a boycott of the Campbell's Soup Company, which uses much of the Ohio tomato crop in catsup, tomato sauce, and, of course, soup. Velasquez argues that Campbell's has used mechanization as a way to limit farm-worker demands by threatening to demand that farmers mechanize to achieve higher yields per acre, thereby eliminating jobs for manual workers. In fact, mechanization has been steadily increasing so that currently 90 percent of the Ohio tomato crop is harvested by machine.

FLOC has organized strikes against growers who supply Campbell's and other food processors, and it has published posters and other materials urging consumers not to buy Campbell's products until conditions for the thousands of migrant workers who harvest tomatoes and cucumbers in the Middle West are improved. FLOC's position is that since Campbell's determines the price it will pay for the crops, Campbell's in effect determines what the growers, mostly small farmers, can or will pay the workers or spend on worker housing.

Campbell's, for its part, claims it has no direct responsibility for workers' conditions, since it buys from the growers on a contract basis. The company points out that since it is the growers who hire the workers, the growers are the employers to whom complaints about labor conditions should be made. In 1985, however, Campbell's agreed to the establishment of an independent commission to oversee representation elections in the tomato and cucumber fields of Ohio and Michigan. In February 1986 a historic, three-party, collective bargaining agreement was signed by Campbell's, the tomato and cucumber growers supplying Campbell's and its subsidiaries, and FLOC.

The Outlook

Given the complexity of contemporary U.S. agriculture, the situation of the farm workers is also complex. Those who own the land are themselves at the mercy of large forces—the pressures of industrialization and the market—rendering the condition of those who work the land the owners' last and least concern.

As agriculture in the United States is practiced on an increasingly large, industrial scale, farmers will try to cut costs and improve efficiency by technology and mechanization. In the process the relation between the individual farmer and his particular acres of land and crew of workers will become more indirect, impersonal, and standardized, more like management-worker relations in factories. This trend could, however, help farmers if it led to their being afforded through collective bargaining the same benefits and redress of grievances as other industrial workers.

Other aspects of industrialization are more problematic. Greater use of pesticides is not only hazardous to workers but reduces the need for some jobs, such as hoeing weeds. Mechanization has reduced the need for year-round workers, such as tractor drivers, and eliminated the need for much seasonal hand labor in cotton, grain crops, olives, and pickles. The decrease in jobs, however, has leveled off since the late 1970s; seasonal labor will continue to be needed for many crops as far as can be foreseen.

Still other forces affect the farm worker. Although large amounts of U.S. grain are sold abroad, more and more other agricultural products are entering the country from Latin America and the Middle East, reducing the market for domestic crops and the need for workers. Citrus imports from Brazil, for example, have put many Florida orchards out of business and pickers out of work. At the same time, foreign workers willing to work for less pour into the country and compete for what jobs there are.

Caught in these inexorable currents, farm workers have few alternatives. They can continue to fight for the right to be unionized and to press for higher wages, better housing, and greater fringe benefits more in keeping with those of other U.S. workers. Many will do so, of course, although if they ask too much they may be replaced by less-demanding foreign immigrants, who seem likely always to be available.

Many farm workers choose to change their lives by leaving farm work altogether. Some find jobs in packing or food-processing plants. Others join the urban poor. Indeed it is rare to meet farm workers who encourage their children to stay with the farm-worker way of life, and the children talk of a future without farm work.

Meanwhile, until the farm workers can improve their lot in the fields or succeed in leaving them, they continue to suffer the pressures of the varied forces that shape farm work in the United States. As they labor, the eyes of individual farm workers cannot help but seek justice in our own.

A CLOSER VIEW

The Road

The idea is to get to the field; the way doesn't matter—cars and trucks hot from a lot of driving, with too few seats for too many people, or rattling buses owned by growers who have imported workers, who, as they look out of the bus window, do not know where they are, only that they have arrived in America.

Then there is "day haul," the long morning's wait for a ride to work. In Immakolee, Florida, in the heart of the "black gold" muckland area, where in winter much of the nation's fresh produce grows, a yellow school bus swings into the parking lot of a small shopping mall and flaps open its rubber accordion door as it comes to a stop in front of a line of black and Hispanic men. The crew leader stands around, filling one bus after another with the hopeless and the unemployed, who bring themselves to the appointed spot morning after morning to see if there will be a job that day or the next.

The bus fills its seats, takes on standees, and pulls out, leaving about fifty more men behind. Another bus, its door missing altogether, roars into the lot, and without stopping its engine, the driver takes on about twenty men until he shouts, "No more." One last man steps up into the bus, but he is thrown backwards as the bus turns away.

Most of the men wear blue jeans and tee shirts; some also wear cowboy hats or baseball caps. They work Immakolee every winter, they say, but one man remarks, "Them freezes gettin' to be too many to make it worth comin' here." An hour passes and no crew buses arrive, though several buses drive by on the road, already apparently full. "That's shit," a thin black man complains, the irises of his eyes pitch dark, the eyeballs tinged with yellow. "They supposed to pick up in *this* parking lot today!"

The men for whom there is no bus shift their weight from one foot to the other, and exchange very few words. If a bus has not come for them by now, no bus will come. By 9 A.M., it is clear this will be a day without work.

For some crops, the road begins on city streets in the dead of night. In Philadelphia at 3:30 A.M., a new group of "others," southeast Asians, waits for the day-haul bus to take them to pick blueberries in the fields of New Jersey. They huddle according to their languages—Thais here, Laotians opposite, Vietnamese and Cambodians there and there, each group on its own corner of the intersection. Few speak English. They crouch on the cracked sidewalk to sit and wait, as though in an Asian field. They wear many colorful scarves and shawls wrapped around their necks and faces. The children, some no taller than fire hydrants, carry plastic sand pails with string handles in which to collect blueberries. A bus pulls into the intersection; one whole huddle of people rises to clamber aboard. But the bus is already full. The huddle crouches low again to wait.

In the fields, Quintana, a Hispanic crew leader, counts the number of Asians who step out of his bus. They say only one hesitating word, "Here?"

"Yes, yes, yes," answers Quintana, as he slaps his palm to the outstretched palm of an Asian whom he recognizes. "Back again," comments Quintana. "Yes, again, here," answers the picker as his feet hit the earth. Some Hispanic crew leaders think the Asians are Japanese, so they call them "Atom Bombs."

Orchards
Yakima Valley, Oregon 1984

**Migrant, moving on
Sunnyside, Oregon 1982**

**Migrant family on the road
Immokalee, Florida 1982**

**Haitian pepper picker
Sampson County
North Carolina 1981**

"No Picker Needed"
Hood River, Oregon 1980

Undocumented alien
hiding from border patrol
U.S.-Mexican border 1980

Apprehension of
undocumented alien
U.S.-Mexican border 1983

The Workers

At the orange grove on "The ridge" near Wauchula, Florida, day-haul buses drive up under the trees. The bright fruit hangs like ornaments against the dark green leaves, and there is the strong smell of citrus like orange-water perfume. The workers wear long, heavy burlap sacks strapped to their necks, which weigh ninety pounds or so when full. They pull the fruit with either hand and toss one orange, then another, into their sacks. They lose their footing in the sandy ground as the sack grows heavier. Unloading means undoing the neck strap of the sack and letting the oranges fall slowly into bins like a cascade of orange tennis balls. The workers are earning fifty cents for a box of oranges; they do not stop picking.

Some bury their faces and arms among the branches, hunting for oranges as though searching for the secrets of the tree. It is hot inside the boughs, perhaps 95 degrees or so, and buggy outside, as the workers slap off mosquitoes and flies in between handling oranges. When the weather has been hot and dry, the sulfur used to control fruit rot does not wash away. The pickers emerge from the trees with eyes tearing, as if oranges, like onions, could make one cry.

The tomato harvest in Ohio begins in midsummer. These are cannery tomatoes bound to be processed rather than eaten whole. The vines lie like wiring on the ground, along the tops of flat furrows. Workers, hunched at the waist, advance up the rows, straddling three feet to work both sides of the row at once. Rubber buckets are placed strategically throughout the field, so as to be nearby and ready. The workers are jubilant when they find tomatoes on the ground, which have fallen off the plants on their own, for these can be scooped up with two hands and tossed ten at a time into the hampers. These are like money found.

In a tomato field in Florida, about fifty workers, male and female and ten or twelve children, spread out among the plants. It is a school holiday. Each worker carries a long, rubber laundry bucket that will hold about thirty pounds of tomatoes. When the buckets are full, the men will hoist them up on their shoulders, run to the truck waiting at the end of the row, climb on the bumper, dump the load, then run back to their place and start picking again.

The tomatoes are tight on the vine, and the workers push with their thumbs to dislodge them. If any stem adheres, it will cut into the skin of the tomatoes in the bucket and ruin them. Workers are not paid for ruined tomatoes, so the pressure is to pick fast, pick stemless, and pick whole. The plants are prickly; thumbs begin to hurt.

As each load is dumped in the truck, the crew leader's wife—a hefty woman wearing a red bandanna sitting on the roof of the truck as though on a tomato throne—drops a scalloped metal chip into the empty buckets to be turned in for pay at the end of the day. Workers retrieve those chips immediately and thrust them into a pocket, lest they get lost. The father of a boy about twelve is handed his son's first chip for safekeeping, but the boy puts out his hand without missing a step on the way back to their row. The father, sensing that his son well understands that work and money are the same in the fields, places the chip in the boy's outstretched palm. He carefully pockets his chip and reaches into the tomato plants again.

A handful of silver chips is an average adult's full day's work—forty buckets at thirty-five cents each, $14 the worker may never see in cash because workers often pay crew leaders for their food or gas. Chips are both work receipts and money, the currency of the field.

Blueberries are deep, frosty, purple blue, and perfectly round, like marbles. The workers finger them delicately, earning $2.20 to $2.60 to pick a flat—twelve pints. Being careful but being fast, a worker might earn $20 or $25 a day in the 98 degree heat. It takes picking fourteen flats a day to make the equivalent of the minimum wage, or $3.35 an hour.

The berries are fragile, small, and hard to pick. Nimble fingers pay off. Most blueberries are still gathered by hand, but sophisticated machinery is also used. Near Hammonton, New Jersey, in the Pine Barrens, where blueberry bushes line the roads, two black women stop their car to watch a blueberry machine at work. Blacks used to pick the blueberries. These women, too, used to pick.

The machine has two rotary blades, which spin through the plants, gently knocking ripe berries onto a grate. The rotaries jiggle with just the right strength to knock off the ripe and leave the unready to ripen. Sometimes, however, unripe berries fall. The machine feeds the berries through a light sensor, which sorts, by gauging the color, the ripe from the unripe, which are channeled to the ground. Such a machine requires a driver and one other worker to replace approximately eighteen people, picking about 1,500 pounds of berries an hour.

The two black women stare at the machine, their wise, ebony faces analyzing the sight before them. "I never thought they could make a machine that could pick better than we did," one woman says. "Yeah," the other answers, "but I don't miss pickin' in this heat." "Me neither," the first woman agrees, "but what about all those Chinese people they got down here? Wonder what they are going to do now these machines are workin' these bushes?" Her friend is reassuring—"They will probably send the Chinese back to China if it ever comes to that."

The Cascade Mountains divide watery, rainy, western Washington state from the dry desert area of the east. But through irrigation, the Yakima Valley grows it all—hops for beer in great ropes like giant grape vines in early March, asparagus in April, and cherries and apples and other fruit through the year.

Asparagus must be cut by hand. The early golden light of the morning pours off the scrubby hills onto the fields as workers scan them for asparagus stalks ready to cut. Each worker wears a box strapped to the waist and carries a wooden tool about ten inches long, a handle with a blade jutting from its end, like a sharp spatula. An expert cutter moves swiftly from one side of a row to the other, working diagonally so as not to miss a ready stalk, for a stalk left one day too long in the ground will have too much waste on it and won't be paid for. Waste weight, tough ends, is deducted from the total weight the cutter brings in, although the packing companies often sell the waste to local farmers for pig and cattle food. So, on the one hand, a cutter keeps the waste question well in mind. On the other hand, the worker must leave just the right amount of stalk under the earth so that the root will not dry out and the asparagus plant will grow again. Farmers charge the workers for damaged plants.

To pick asparagus, the worker bends at the waist, gripping the top of the stalk, then digs the blade beneath the earth, cutting the stalk off with an audible crunch. At the end of a row, the worker crouches, putting the blade across the knee to resharpen it against a file many carry. Cutting asparagus is a constant rhythm of bend, cut, crunch, and sharpen. Toward the end of the day, when a field has been pretty well picked clean, to avoid the pain of straightening up between stalks and cuts, workers remain bent, moving like hunchbacks through the field.

At the packing plant, it is asparagus everywhere, as women stand in front of squeaking conveyor belts carrying asparagus by size—seven inches on one belt, eight and nine inches on the others. The women are on their feet all day, sorting beneath a row of bare, white light bulbs. They are forbidden to talk to one another, and two foremen move through the aisles, watching, counting, sampling each crate to make sure that there is no damage as the asparagus move along the belts. For the women, it is like spending a day arranging pencils, all points at one end, erasers at the other. "It is very dull," one woman remarked. "If I could I would sleep standing up. But," she added, "this sure beats cuttin' em. I'll never go back to that."

Cherry trees are lush and beautiful, marching up the Yakima hills. Sunlight falls through the branches, and catches on a cluster of cherries hanging as elegantly on the tree as they sit in Picasso's painting of three stemmed cherries on a crisp, white plate. The workers fan out among the trees looking for places to raise their ladders without leaning them against the small fruit. There are a few cherries here, a few there, but no great quantities on one branch, so the ladders must be moved many times. Moving the boughs creates the only breeze in the grove, and the temperature hovers in the upper 80's.

A young woman with thick, black hair running like silk down her neck, stops picking in order to tie her hair up in her bandanna. Then she begins picking again. It is tricky work, for cherries are fragile. "Milked" berries, that is, stemmed at picking, will not be paid for. Nor will cracked cherries, even if they cracked naturally in the sun. Picking is a matter of, rustling branches, lovingly handling the cherries into a sack, then gently rolling them into a crate. For all this expert attention, pickers are paid ten cents a pound.

It is a sunny day, and the trees rustle and sound like big animals walking through a forest. Someone is singing. The trees are covered with shiny, white pesticide powder, and the orchard smells like a pharmacy, despite the presence of so much fruit. A boy, about thirteen, tries to hold his nose with one hand and grab cherries from a branch with the other.

35¢ for twelve bunches
green onion field
Salt River Valley, Arizona 1979

Pear picker
Lake County, California 1979

Hoer, pepper field
Merced, California 1983

**Young onion picker
Rio Grande Valley, Texas 1979**

Campesino
Salt River Valley, Arizona 1980

Field latrines
Hillsboro, Oregon 1982

Tractor driver, asparagus field
Sacramento Delta, California 1982

Cherry picker
Sunnyside, Washington 1982

**Haitian field worker
Immokalee, Florida 1982**

Lunchtime, pear orchard
Hood River, Oregon 1980

Breakfast in a cucumber field
Northwest Ohio 1980

Break in the fields
Rio Grande Valley, Texas 1979

Setting asparagus
Sherman Island
Sacramento Delta, California 1982

Lettuce picker
corporate farm
Salinas, California 1983

Corn picker
Rio Grande Valley, Texas 1979

Potato picker
Northwest Ohio 1980

Undocumented worker
picking pears
Lake County, California 1979

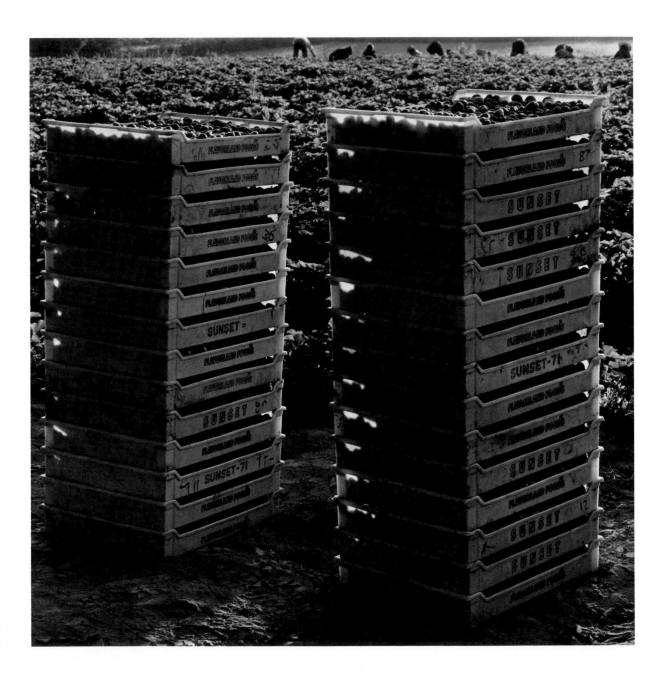

Strawberries, $1.50 a flat
Hillsboro, Oregon 1982

**Grape picker
Delano, California 1982**

Grape picker
Napa Valley, California 1984

Picking cucumbers
Northwest Ohio 1980

Children in the Fields

"The worst thing is in the morning when the plants are wet and your hands get cold. Here, feel my hands." They are damp, yet soft, the fragile fingers of Martina, an eight-year-old picker with blonde hair braided by her mother at 6:00 A.M. before the family began their day in the northern California strawberry field. The leaves of the plants are deep green, and the berries are as richly red as the dirt is brown. There are five children and two adults, share-cropping strawberries here with other families who do not own the land they work, nor do they own the plywood boxes, the "flats," they fill with berries.

All men in the strawberry field wear hats or caps of some kind, advertising a baseball team, a type of farm equipment, something to drink. The women wear colorful kerchiefs up over their noses and around the backs of their necks to protect them from cold, dust, and bugs, and they swirl the cloths up and into place in one graceful movement, like veiled Islamic women going into hiding. Sometimes workers make protective garments out of bags for packing produce—shawls of burlap, vests of sacking—when weather suddenly gets cold or windy or wet.

Martina sits on her haunches, pushing her flat ahead of her as she moves along on her knees. She tries to shake the cold from her fingers. No one uses gloves, for picking strawberries requires dexterity and finger control. She points to her stained hands. "That redness won't come out.... we use Chlorox and shampoo, and sometimes it helps but sometimes it stays for a long time." The family picks strawberries for canneries rather than the table market, which means that the strawberry stems must be removed.

"It's easier when we pick for the market," Martina's mother explains, wiping some hair from her eye with the back of a hand full of strawberries, because "we don't have to pull off the green then." Another worker fiddles too long with a berry stem and Martina strolls over. "If it is hard, you can just cut it like this." She plunges her small thumb through the crown of the berry and flips the fruit into the flat. She has been picking berries for two years. "It is boring," she observes, "and I don't like it."

Anelia, a short, round woman with a magnificent gracious spirit, sits at her formica kitchen table in the middle of the large room where her entire family sleeps when they are working the tomato harvest. Her husband, Romero, drives a tractor in Texas in winter, but because there isn't enough year-round work there, they migrate to Ohio, by car and pickup truck, to harvest the small cucumbers they call "pickles" and then tomatoes.

They are eight—Roberto, age thirteen, Alejandro, age twelve, their parents, their younger sister, their older sister and her husband, and their newborn niece. Though the quarters are cramped, Anelia can keep them clean. And she is glad to be where they are, recounting the days "before this farmer, when we lived in camps with mattresses on the floor, no sheets, and it was never clean."

Anelia, who came from Mexico, only finished third grade, but she encourages her youngest children to do well at school. She tries not to leave Texas until they have finished the school year. When there is a little bit of extra money, her husband or oldest son comes to Ohio ahead of the family to be sure they do not miss out on a place in the "good" camp. She wants her children to study hard so "they will not always have to be pickers." In Texas, the boys go to the fields for an hour or so after school, except when they have a lot of homework, but they spend their entire summer vacation at work in Ohio.

Anelia, like most farm-worker women, is the heart of the home. She wakes everybody up about 6 A.M., having herself risen at 4 A.M. to prepare breakfast. In less than ten minutes, she has a dozen tortillas piled on plates, milk warming, coffee brewing, eggs, and, sometimes, sausage, simmering. Then she packs the family's lunch to be eaten in the field, and goes off with the family to pick until about 6 P.M., preceding the men back to camp. She showers, prepares dinner, and somehow also finds time to launder and press everybody's clothes. The family works every day except Sundays, weather permitting. Since they have no medical insurance, they hope for good health so they can keep on working in the fields.

When asked what her dreams are, Anelia says she wishes only that her children will grow up to be healthy and happy, that she will live long enough to be able to advise them through life's difficulties, and that she will also live long enough to take care of her elderly aunt.

All the pressure to plan and juggle money falls on Anelia and her husband. It is they who know that replacing a ripped pair of rubber work gloves can mean one less quart of milk that week. Romero is in his fifties but looks seventy. His face is not just lined, but worn, although his eyes sparkle when he speaks of his wife, whom he calls "my diamond, my flower." If there were work enough in Texas, they would stay there. They do not like to migrate.

The tomato fields can be muddy and wet, so everyone in the family wears rubber boots. In the morning, Alejandro retrieves his from under the cabin where he keeps them at night. He rests them on the floor and with practiced fingers wraps the bottoms of his trousers with rubber bands as if he were going long-distance bicycling. Then he pulls on the boots, which are a bit too big. As he walks they scuff along the wood floor, and so the prevailing morning sounds in the cabin are rubber boots against wood and the rolling pin being pushed back and forth on fresh tortillas by Anelia.

The boys look like little boys anywhere, except that they try to do the day's work of an adult every day. In the fields, Alejandro is still too short to be able to straddle a row, and his older brother reprimands him from time to time for stepping on tomatoes. "Stay in the furrow, Alejandro," Roberto says.

When asked what he thinks about while at work in the fields, Alejandro gazes out over the spotted red earth and answers, "Nothing…work…tomatoes!" The sight of so many thousands of tomatoes still to pick makes one vow never to eat catsup again. Alejandro quips, "Fortunately, I prefer mustard."

Because entire families are picking usually, and there are few day-care facilities for farm-worker children, toddlers and infants grow up in the fields while their parents labor. Babies are nursed in the field; children are bathed there.

In a tomato field, two children sit in the dirt, one a toddler apparently in the charge of his older sister, Jeannette. She is eight years old, and she has been picking a little since early morning. She has filled eight baskets, called hampers – "one for each of my birthday years," she reported with a smile. She has stopped because she was tired. Her brother does not pick yet, she says, because he is too little. Her eyes are wide and bright and she sits on the fringes of the field, drawing circles in the dirt with a castoff green tomato as though it were a crayon.

Maria, age nine, the daughter of orange pickers and tomato pickers, is a third-generation migrant child, who has stood on the tops of cars waving United Farm Worker flags during strikes in the fields. She has an adult's view of the world. When asked why farm workers have such continuing struggle, she hesitates only briefly in her reply: "They think we are nothing, just like a piece of stick or a rock or something. But we aren't nothing; we are like them, people."

In the early evening, children play touch football with a giant cucumber that was left growing on a vine too long. Most of the children have been working all day. Vicki, age twelve, has been picking for two seasons. She has long, black hair and a beautiful, Modigliani face. Her older sister has a job working a mechanical harvester, so Vicki hopes it will stop raining because the machines cannot negotiate the wet fields and then there will be no work. When her sister is not working, she is not getting paid. Vicki sweeps the steps of her family's cabin wearing an orange satin party dress; it is all she has besides her field clothes.

Margarita, age nine, has been overtaken by age rather than puberty. Her eyes have no light in them, it seems. She picks a little in the mornings and tidies her family's shack every afternoon. Here, garbage is collected once a week if that, and the window screens would more aptly be called rusted wiring. Margarita sweeps, scooping up dust and dirt into an empty pesticide bucket and then pouring it into a larger receptacle supplied by the farmer, which quickly fills. She looks forlornly at the tomato fields next to her camp and shakes her head "no" when asked if there is anything good to be said about picking.

Johnny, about twelve, sits on the grass in front of the shell of a house in which his family is expected to live. He says he has been "coming and going since I was born." In summer school in Ohio, he bucks prejudice. "They say you are from Mexico, you know, but I am not, and at night sometimes you hear cars with people yelling, 'Hey migrants get out of here'....they should be at least glad because we are doing some work for them. If it wasn't for us, there would be no tomatoes, no sugar beets, no sugar, no pickles. They should pay attention, but they just say, 'Get out of here.'"

Child of the fields
Rio Grande Valley, Texas 1979

**Laotian family
strawberry harvest, $1.50 a flat
Hillsboro, Oregon 1982**

**Bath in the tomato fields
Northwest Ohio 1980**

**Child sleeping in car
as parents pick blueberries
Hammonton, New Jersey 1981**

7:00 A.M., green onion field
Salt River Valley, Arizona 1979

Seven-year-old boy
paid 30¢ a bucket
Leipsic, Ohio 1980

Child of migrant pear pickers
Lake County, California 1979

The Crops

There is a lot of beauty in the fields, as sun falls on the shining skins of fruits and vegetables, and neat rows of plants lend a comforting order to the land, against the confused sound of truck engines and radios and workers yelling one to the other to pass a bucket or a drink of water.

There is beauty too in bunches of grapes tapering perfectly toward the ground as though designed in porcelain, or in sheafs of green onions tied and placed one over the other, almost woven together.

But it is the measuring, not the beauty, that counts in the fields. Crops by the bucket, the bag, the flat, the box, the pail, the basket – onions picked and put into bags so they can be weighed, then spilled out and piled loose into trucks for shipment.

Every crop is different, every fruit or vegetable has its own way of being harvested, its own need to be protected. Growers sometimes depict crops painted with smiling faces to sell produce, but every worker gauges feelings about the crops in relationship to what it takes to pick them.

"The best thing about picking is finishing," a young worker said. She had particular comments about cucumbers. "The worst thing is when cucumbers for pickles get all yellow and mushy, and you touch them by mistake. Pickles are harder than tomatoes, because you have to turn the plants back the way they were, so new pickles will grow. In tomatoes, you don't have to turn the plants over. And you can see where you stopped because you just pick the red ones – all you can get."

Grapes
Delano, California 1982

Two ladders at dusk pear orchard
Hood River, Oregon 1980

Melon picker
Northwest Ohio 1980

Green onions
Salt River Valley, Arizona 1979

"Danger/Peligro"
Salinas, California 1983

Roadside sign
Homestead, Florida 1982

Cherries
Yakima Valley, Washington 1982

Cannery workers
Rio Grande Valley, Texas 1979

Processing plant
Winter Haven, Florida 1982

**Packing shed worker
Rio Grande Valley, Texas 1979**

Home

It is hard when you have no choice about what is home, and worse when after a day of heavy work, the home you have is crowded and hot and cannot be properly cleaned. Rest from labor, peace and quiet, cannot be had in such a home.

In Ohio, a migrant family was expected to live in the ruins of a house that had been burned by vandals during the winter, or find work elsewhere. Although the farmer-owner had made no repairs, the place had somehow passed state inspection for farm-worker housing. (The youngest family member thought maybe the farmer and the inspector had done "money talks.") The family made the interior livable at their own expense, but the exterior still bore scars of the fire. The frame was exposed in places, and there was no insulation except some wispy puffs that lingered in parts of the wall. The nearest drinkable water was a mile and a half away, but that was true before the fire.

According to Johnny, age twelve, "Every migrant has the same problems – rats, and torn cushions. When they get here, the first thing they do is put out rat traps or rat poison and clean up their place."

A farm worker who had been coming to Ohio since the age of thirteen, nearly twenty-five years, sat on a maroon armchair, which oozed it stuffing, and said, "Just look around." A bare mattress stained by dirt and years of use rested on four concrete blocks. "In this camp," he said, "no one drinks the water. There is no place to take an inside shower. When we arrive every year, the place is too dirty–filthy. I am ashamed to bring my family here, but I have no choice. The farmer knows about it, but he does nothing."

In Wauchula, Florida, a farm-labor camp consisted of one long bunkhouse with several rooms. Unmarked dirt roads led to it, and no main road could be seen from it. A one-armed black man stood in the kitchen, which was nothing more than a propane tank and one gas burner on a wooden table with three legs and a stick of wood for the fourth. The man stirred a thick, brown stew, which he ate from the saucepan still sitting on the burner because it was the only eating arrangement he could manage with one arm. In the next room, the communal toilet was caked with human excrement. A black man wearing no shirt and stained chino pants tried to flush it with a bucket of water. In a large bedroom, none of the six cots had sheets to cover the thin mattresses.

Outside, two men, also black, sat on metal folding chairs around a card table, drinking beer and complaining about the heat. They had been recruited on the streets of Miami to pick oranges and dropped off at the camp by their crew leader, whom they knew only as "Joe." They had not started picking yet, but Joe had begun charging their room and board against monies they had not yet earned. "That Joe charges a dollar for a beer," one of the men remarked, and added, "Nobody in Miami knows I am here. Maybe that's why I'm here."

The one-armed man shouted over from the kitchen, "Bossman Joe says we'll be doing oranges soon, so don't go away."

"Ain't thinkin' about leavin' cause I can't leave," came the reply from the man at the card table as he swigged his beer.

Migrant shacks
edge of tomato field
Northwest Ohio 1980

**Washing for dinner
migrant camp
Hood River, Oregon 1980**

Cabin 34, migrant camp
Delano, California 1982

Mother and child
labor camp
Yakima, Washington 1982

On the doorstep
migrant camp
Northwest Ohio 1980

Migrant child, third generation
migrant camp
Merced, California 1983

**Migrant farm worker
labor camp
Merced, California 1983**

**Tomato picker
migrant camp
Northwest Ohio 1980**

Haitian farm-worker family
Blockers Camp
Immokalee, Florida 1982

**Dinner, migrant camp
Merced, California 1983**

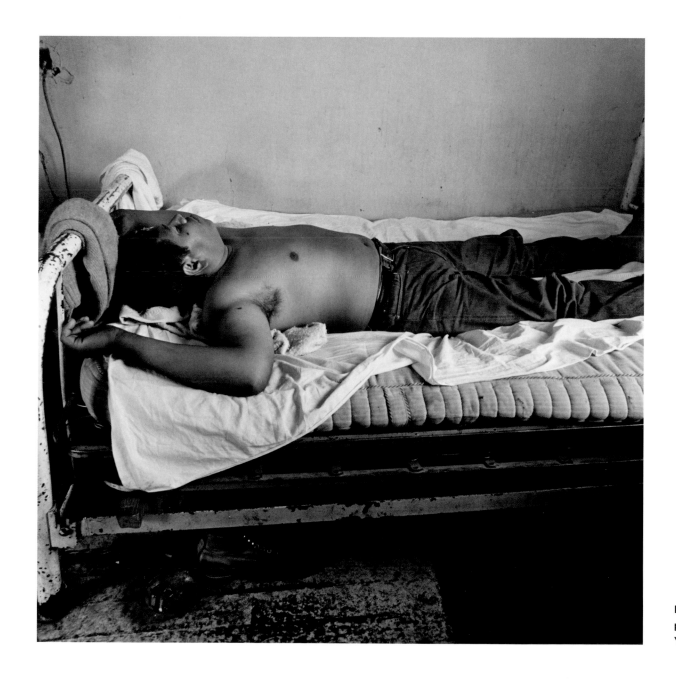

End of long day
picking cherries, labor camp
Yakima, Washington 1982

Sleeping under
the orange trees
Salt River Valley, Arizona 1979

End of the cucumber harvest
packing for the trip to Indiana
Northwest Ohio 1980

THE MEANS OF CHANGE

Once people are aware of the situation of farm workers, which has remained so desperate for so long, it is to be hoped that they will want to help to bring about change. The agency that has worked longest, more than sixty-five years, and most consistently to improve living conditions and conditions in the fields is the National Farm Worker Ministry. It is composed of forty-five national religious organizations and is related to the National Council of Churches.

The National Farm Worker Ministry spent its first forty years in charitable and benevolent direct services, collecting food and clothing for farm workers and creating health clinics and child-care centers. During that time, its members saw little change in the American agricultural system. Farm workers continued poor and oppressed and exploited. As the father of one mushroom-picking family in eastern Pennsylvania told a minister and parishioners bringing a traditional Thanksgiving basket to his home, "Reverend, just once I'd like to have enough money to buy my own turkey!" No matter how well-intentioned, charity does little more than make the giver feel good and create dependency in the recipient.

In 1962, when Cesar Chavez organized farm workers into what became the United Farm Workers union and struck the vineyards of California, the National Farm Worker Ministry intentionally chose to use its limited resources to support the workers' efforts. Thus church people were pulled into a new form of ministry. Chavez' policy of workers' self-determination based on the principle of nonviolence put those who wanted to help in the position of servanthood, not merely service. Instead of saying, "Here, have some of our abundance in your poverty," the NFWM said. "Tell us what you need. We will try to respond."

What the farm workers asked for, of course, was the presence of NFWM representatives on the picket line, resources for the strike, and ultimately support for the boycott of grapes. That boycott and later others borrowed economic power from consumers to empower farm workers to make demands, and they involved consumers themselves in activity that made them part of a solution, rather than putting a bandaid on the problem. Thus the boycotts provided a uniquely effective tool in the struggle for justice in the fields.

Since then the National Farm Worker Ministry has continued to support the United Farm Workers (UFW). It also supports the Farm Labor Organizing Committee (FLOC), a similar, more recently formed, movement by midwestern tomato and cucumber pickers. The NFWM places a majority of its staff directly within these farm workers' organizations and supports them at subsistence level. These "worker-priests/sisters" commit their skills and energies, representing one part of the church that believes such action is one way to put love at work in the world.

The **National Farm Worker Ministry** seeks resources to support the staff who work directly with the farm workers. Also it offers information and speakers to interpret farm-worker needs to religious and civic organizations. Its offices are located at

111-A Fairmount Avenue, Oakland, Calif. 94611 Tel. (415) 465-3264

2701 West Chicago Boulevard, Detroit, Mich. 48206 Tel. (313) 868-2724

P.O. Box 5024, Tampa, Fla. 33675 Tel. (813) 223-2141

Individuals can aid the workers' cause in many ways. They can contribute money to their churches or directly to the NFWM. They can volunteer for full-time service within the farm workers' organizations. Those who would like to do so are directed to the following addresses:

United Farm Workers, La Paz, Calif. 93570 Tel. (805) 822-5571

Farm Labor Organizing Committee, 714½ South St. Clair Street, Toledo, Ohio 43609 Tel. (419) 243-3456

Within the UFW and FLOC, people are needed as community organizers for boycotts in urban areas; as managers in field offices and service centers; as health-care givers in clinics; as administrators of finance, health, and pension plans; and as clerical and legal assistants.

On a less involved level, individuals can support the unions' boycotts of various crops. In early 1986 there were three boycotts in support of the farm workers' cause: nonunion table grapes, Red Coach label iceberg lettuce, and Chiquita bananas—sponsored by the UFW.

There continues to be strong need for many direct services, especially in parts of the country where workers are not yet being organized. Thus, there are ample opportunities for people who would prefer helping in that way. Some recommended organizations are listed on the following pages.

Organizations

Bishops' Committee on Migration
1312 Massachusetts Avenue
NW Washington, DC 20005
(202) 659-6681
Adjunct to U.S. Catholic Conference of Bishops
dealing with pastoral care of immigrants and
refugees.

California Rural Legal Assistance
2111 Mission, San Francisco, CA 94110
(415) 864-3405
Independently funded legal agency that files class
action suits, and otherwise acts as legal advocate,
for farm workers in matters such as pesticide
protection and mechanization.

East Coast Farmworker Support Network
P.O. Box 1633, Raleigh, NC 27602
(919) 682-3818
Network of organizations acting as advocate for
farm workers along the East Coast.

Farmworker Justice Fund
2001 "S" Street, NW Washington, DC 20009
(202) 462-8192
Gathers and disseminates information, especially
about legislation, pertaining to farm workers.

Florida IMPACT
222 West Pensacola, Tallahassee, FL 32301
(904) 222-3470
Church-sponsored legislative advocate for farm-
worker concerns in health, safety, and collective
bargaining.

Illinois Farm Worker Ministry
935 Curtiss Street, Rm. 8, Downers Grove, IL 60515
Church-sponsored ministry of advocacy for farm
workers in Illinois.

Indiana Farm Worker Ministry
1100 West 42nd Street, Rm. 225
Indianapolis, IN 46208
Church-sponsored ministry of advocacy for farm
workers in Indiana.

Michigan Farm Worker Ministry Coalition
2701 West Chicago Blvd., Detroit, MI 48206
(313) 883-6959
Church-sponsored ministry of advocacy for farm
workers in Michigan.

Migrant Legal Action Program
2001 "S" Street, NW Washington, DC 20009
(202) 462-7744
Gathers and disseminates information, especially
about legal activity on behalf of farm workers.

National Migrant Worker Council
539 West Berry Street, Fort Wayne, IN 46802
Federally sponsored network of health-care givers
and advocates.

Triangle Friends of the Farm Workers
2722 McDowell Street, Durham, NC 27705
(919) 489-2659
Religious- and labor-based group of advocates for
farm workers in North Carolina.

Resources

Books for Adults

Barrio, Raymond. *The Plum Pickers.* Sunnyvale, Calif.: Ventura Press, 1969. Paper. A novel of a migrant family.

Coles, Robert. *Uprooted Children.* New York: Harper & Row, 1970.

Forbes, Jack B. *Aztecas del Norte: The Chicanos of Aztlan.* Greenwich, Conn.: Fawcett Publications, 1973.

Goldfarb, Ronald L. *A Caste of Despair.* Ames: Iowa State Univ. Press, 1981. Most recent, factual history of the farm workers' movement analyzing the effects of reforms.

Johnston, Helen. *Health for the Nation's Harvesters.* Farmington Hills, Mich.: National Migrant Worker Council, 1985.

Kushner, Sam. *Long Road to Delano.* New York: International Publisher, 1968.

Levy, Jacques E. *Cesar Chavez: Autobiography of La Causa.* New York: W.W. Norton, 1975.

Matthiessen, Peter. *Sal Si Puedes: Cesar Chavez and the New American Revolution.* New York: Random House, 1969.

Meister, Richard, and Loftis, Ann. *A Long Time Coming.* New York: Macmillan, 1977.

Migrant Women Speak. New York: World Council of Churches.

Smith, Patrick D. *Angel City.* St. Petersburg, Fla.: Valkyrie Publishers, 1978. Novel of a family in a southern Florida migrant camp.

Taylor, Ronald B. *Chavez and the Farm Workers.* Boston: Beacon Press, 1975.

Taylor, Ronald B. *Sweatshop in the Sun.* Boston: Beacon Press, 1973. A study of child labor on the farm.

Books for Children

Crawford, Ann Fears, and Chapa, Pedro, Jr. *Viva: Famous Mexican Americans.* 1976.

Franchere, Ruth. *Cesar Chavez.* New York: Crowell, 1970.

Immel, Mary Blair. *Call Up the Thunder.* St. Louis: Bethany Press, 1969.

Smith, Nancy S. *Josie's Handfull of Quietness.* Nashville: Abingdon Press.

"Teaching About the Rights of Children," teaching packet #5417, U.S. Committee for UNICEF, 331 East 38th Street, New York, N.Y. 10016.

A United Farm Workers Union Coloring Book with Spanish/English captions. United Farm Workers, La Paz, Keene, Calif. 93531

White, Florence M. *Cesar Chavez, Man of Courage.* New Canaan, Conn.: Garrad Publishing Co., 1973.

Articles and Booklets

Determining Our Destiny: Agriculture and Farm Labor in Florida. Florida Catholic Conference, P.O. Box 1571, Tallahassee, Fla. 32302. 14-page information and study questions and additional "Resource Bibliography."

The Church, Growers, and Farm Workers. Shalom Task Force, Church of Brethren, P.O. Box 296, St. Cloud, Fla. 32769. 1977.

Agribusiness Manual. Interfaith Center on Corporate Responsibility, 475 Riverside Drive, Rm. 566, New York, N.Y. 10027. Some 30 articles on corporate responsibility and hunger issues, worldwide. A good buy for serious study.

Florida's Farm Workers…Towards a Responsible Public Policy. Institute for Social Policy Studies, P.O. Box 10111, Tallahassee, Fla. 32302. 1977.

"The Plight of America's 5 Million Migrants." Loretta Schwartz, *Ms,* June 1978.

Caribbean Migration: Contract Labor in U.S. Agriculture. NACLA report, Nov. 1977. North American Congress on Latin America, Box 57, Cathedral Station, N.Y. 10025

The Condition of Farm Workers and Small Farmers in 1975. National Sharecroppers Fund/Rural Advancement Fund, 2128 Commonwealth Avenue, Charlotte, N.C. 28205.

"The Family Farm" and "Farm Labor Unionization," packets on these and related topics. National Farm Worker Ministry, 111-A Fairmount Avenue, Oakland, Calif. 94611.

Promises to Keep: The Continuing Crisis in the Education of Migrant Children. The National Child Labor Committee, 145 East 32nd Street, New York, N.Y. 10016. 1977.

Florida Impact: Farmworkers. National Farm Worker Ministry, P.O. Box 5024, Tampa, Fla. 33675.

Periodicals

Food and Justice. United Farm Workers, La Paz, Calif. 93570.

MLAP Bulletin. Migrant Legal Action Program, 2001 "S" Street, NW Washington, D.C. 20001.

MLAP Field Memo. Migrant Legal Action Program, 2001 "S" Street, NW Washington, D.C. 20001

NFWM Newsletter. National Farm Worker Ministry, 111-A Fairmount Avenue, Oakland, Calif. 94611. Quarterly.

Audiovisuals

Project C.H.A.I.N (Combating Hunger and Injustice Now). National Farm Worker Ministry, P.O. Box 5024, Tampa, Fla. 33675. 40-minute slide-tape program by Faith Presbyterian Church, Dunedin, Fla. Part 1 is an excellent introduction to the farm-worker situation. Part 2 shows the ministry of C.H.A.I.N. 1978.

This Far by Faith. National Farm Worker Ministry, 111-A Fairmount Avenue, Oakland, Calif. 94611. 15-min. slide-tape program by National Farm Worker Ministry, detailing the 60-year history of migrant ministry. 1980.

La Raza: The Mexican-Americans. P.O. Box 5096, Stanford, Conn. 94305. Multimedia production of lessons in Mexican-American history. 1969.

Democracy Where It Matters Most. National Farm Worker Ministry, 111-A Fairmount Avenue, Oakland, Calif. 94611. 12-min. slide-tape program by National Farm Worker Ministry describing how farm workers under contract function in United Farm Worker Ranch Committees. 1978.

Religious Significance of the Farm Workers' Movement. National Farm Worker Ministry, 111-A Fairmount Avenue, Oakland, Calif. 94611. Tape cassette interview with Wayne C. Hartmire, Jr., former director of National Farm Worker Ministry, 1972.

Films

Day Without Sunshine. National Farm Worker Ministry, 111-A Fairmount Avenue, Oakland, Calif. 94611. Documentary color film by WPTB Public TV, Miami, Fla. 1978.

Fighting for Our Lives. National Farm Worker Ministry, 111-A Fairmount Avenue, Oakland, Calif. 94611. 50-min. color film by United Farm Workers, story of the Teamster/UFW struggle in 1973. 1973.

Why We Boycott. 15-min. version of *Fighting for Our Lives.*

Poverty in the Valley of Plenty. National Farm Worker Ministry, P.O. Box 5024, Tampa, Fla. 33675. Film about the DiGiorgio grape strike in 1968. 1974.

Si, Se Puede. National Farm Worker Ministry, 111-A Fairmount Avenue, Oakland, Calif. 94611. 55-min. color film by United Farm Workers, story of Arizona governor's recall campaign and Cesar Chavez' fast of 1972. 1972.

Migrant: An NBC White Paper. USCC Dept. of Social Development, 1312 Massachusetts Avenue, NW Washington, D.C. 20005. 53-min. color film by NBC. 1970.